Thoughts on
PROSPERITY

Thoughts on

PROSPERITY

TRIUMPH BOOKS
CHICAGO

This edition is published by Triumph Books, Chicago,
by arrangement with Forbes Inc.

ISBN 1-57243-107-5 (cloth)

This book is available in quantity at special discounts for your group
or organization. For more information, contact:

TRIUMPH BOOKS
644 South Clark Street
Chicago, Illinois 60605
(312) 939-3330 FAX (312) 663-3557

Book design by Graffolio.
Cover design © 1996 by Triumph Books.
Illustration from the Dover Pictorial Archive Series,
edited by Jim Harter (Dover Publications), used with permission.
Some of the properties in the photograph on the front cover
courtesy of Bloomingdale's.

Printed in the United States of America.

CONTENTS

INTRODUCTION

The moving motive in establishing FORBES Magazine, in 1917, was ardent desire to promulgate humaneness in business, then woefully lacking. . . .

Every issue of FORBES, since its inception, has appeared under the masthead: "With all thy getting, get understanding."

Not only so, but we have devoted, all through the years, a full page to "Thoughts on the Business of Life," reflections by ancient and modern sages calculated to inspire a philosophic mode of life, broad sympathies, charity towards all. . . .

I have faith that the time will eventually come when employees and employers, as well as all mankind, will realize that they serve themselves best when they serve others most.

B. C. Forbes

ABUNDANCE

A man with a surplus
can control circumstances,
but a man without a surplus
is controlled by them,
and often he has no opportunity
to exercise judgment.

HARVEY FIRESTONE

———

Abundance consists not alone
in material possession,
but in an uncovetous spirit.

CHARLES M. SHELDON

———

Be rather bountiful than expensive;
do good with what thou hast,
or it will do thee no good.

WILLIAM PENN

By whatever basis
human desires are classified,
the promise of an abundant life
covers virtually all.
To the spiritual,
it suggests escape from futility;
to the sensuous
it calls up visions of luxury;
to the defeated
it is a dream of success.

CADMAN

I keep the telephone of my mind
open to peace, harmony, health,
love and abundance.
Then, whenever doubt, anxiety,
or fear try to call me,
they keep getting a busy signal—
and they'll soon forget my number.

EDITH ARMSTRONG

Independence may be found
in comparative as well as in absolute abundance;
I mean where a person contracts his desires
within the limits of his fortune.

WILLIAM SHENSTONE

The more you learn
what to do with yourself,
and the more you do for others,
the more you will learn to enjoy
the abundant life.

WILLIAM J. H. BOETCKER

Money and time
are the heaviest burdens of life,
and the unhappiest of all mortals
are those who have more of either
than they know how to use.

SAMUEL JOHNSON

Plenty and indigence
depend upon the opinion
every one has of them;
and riches, like glory or health,
have no more beauty or pleasure
than their possessor
is pleased to lend them.

MICHEL DE MONTAIGNE

———✦———

I hold this to be the rule of life,
"Too much of anything is bad."

TERENCE

———✦———

The life each of us lives
is the life within the limits of our own thinking.
To have life more abundant,
we must think in the limitless terms
of abundance.

THOMAS DREIER

Troubles are usually
the brooms and shovels
that smooth the road
to a good man's fortune;
and many a man curses the rain
that falls upon his head,
and knows not that it brings
abundance to drive away hunger.

ST. BASIL

Wealth is not of necessity a curse,
nor poverty a blessing.
Wholesome and easy abundance
is better than either extreme.

ROSWELL D. HITCHCOCK

AMBITION

Aim at perfection in everything,
though in most things
it is unattainable;
however, they who aim at it,
and persevere,
will come much nearer to it
than those whose laziness
and despondency make them
give it up as unattainable.

LORD CHESTERFIELD

(PHILIP DORMER STANHOPE)

Ambition is most aroused
by the trumpet-clang
of another's fame.

BALTASAR GRACIÁN

Ambition is the germ
from which all growth
of nobleness proceeds.

T. D. ENGLISH

Ambition makes the same mistake
concerning power
that avarice makes as to wealth.
She begins by accumulating it
as a means to happiness,
and finishes by continuing
to accumulate it as an end.

CHARLES CALEB COLTON

If you want to succeed
in the world you must make
your own opportunities as you go on.
The man who waits
for some seventh wave
to toss him on dry land
will find that the seventh wave
is a long time coming.

JOHN B. GOUGH

Money is power.
Every good man and woman
ought to strive for power,
to do good with it
when obtained.
I say, get rich, get rich!

RUSSELL HERMAN CONWELL

Most people
would succeed in small things
if they were not troubled by great ambitions.

HENRY WADSWORTH LONGFELLOW

The road to happiness
lies in two simple principles:
find what it is that interests you
and that you can do well,
and when you find it
put your whole soul into it—
every bit of energy and ambition
and natural ability you have.

JOHN D. ROCKEFELLER III

The tallest trees
are most in the power of the winds,
and ambitious men in the blasts of fortune.

WILLIAM PENN

The slave has but one master;
the man of ambition has
as many as there are people
useful to his fortune.

JEAN DE LA BRUYÈRE

To be ambitious for wealth,
and yet always expecting to be poor;
to be always doubting your ability
to get what you long for,
is like trying to reach east
by traveling west.
There is no philosophy
which will help man to succeed
when he is always doubting
his ability to do so,
and thus attracting failure.

CHARLES BANDOUIN

CHARACTER

A Creed:
To be so strong
that nothing can disturb
your peace of mind;
to talk health, happiness and prosperity;
to make your friends feel
that there is something in them;
to look on the sunny side of everything;
to be too large for worry,
too noble for anger,
too strong for fear,
and too happy
to permit the presence of trouble.

CHRISTIAN D. LARSON

Capitalism
is the only system in the world
founded on credit and character.

HUBERT EATON

A good name is seldom regained.
When character is gone,
all is gone,
and one of the richest jewels of life
is lost forever.

J. HAWES

A man's treatment of money
is the most decisive test of his character—
how he makes it
and how he spends it.

JAMES MOFFATT

A man's true estate of power and riches
is to be in himself;
not in his dwelling or position
or external relations,
but in his own essential character.

HENRY WARD BEECHER

Character and personal force
are the only investments
that are worth anything.

WALT WHITMAN

———

Character is power;
it makes friends,
draws patronage and support,
and opens a sure way
to wealth, honor and happiness.

J. HOWE

———

Fame is a vapor,
popularity an accident,
riches take wings.
Only one thing endures,
and that is character.

HORACE GREELEY

Get to know
two things about a man—
how he earns his money
and how he spends it—
and you have the clue
to his character,
for you have a searchlight
that shows up the inmost recesses
of his soul.

ROBERT JAMES MCCRACKEN

Prosperity cannot be divorced
from humanity.

CALVIN COOLIDGE

I've noticed two things
about men who get big salaries.
They are almost invariably
men who, in conversation
or in conference,
are adaptable.
They quickly get
the other fellow's view.
They are more eager to do this
than to express their own ideas.
Also, they state their own point
of view convincingly.

JOHN HALLOCK

Only what we have wrought
into our character during life
can we take way with us.

ALEXANDER HUMBOLDT

In the long run,
digging for truth
has always proved
not only more interesting
but more profitable
than digging for gold.

GEORGE R. HARRISON

It is fortunate
to be of high birth,
but it is no less
to be of such character
that people do not care to know
whether you are or are not.

JEAN DE LA BRUYÈRE

Nature has written
a letter of credit
upon some men's faces
that is honored wherever presented.
You cannot help trusting such men.
Their very presence gives confidence.
There is "promise to pay" in their faces
which gives confidence
and you prefer it
to another man's endorsement.
Character is credit.

WILLIAM MAKEPEACE THACKERAY

The measure of a man
is not in the number of his servants,
but in the number
of people whom he serves.

PAUL D. MOODY

The abundant life
of which we have heard so much . . .
does not come to those
who have all obstacles removed
from their paths by others.
It develops from within
and is rooted in strong mental
and moral fiber.

WILLIAM MATHER LEWIS

You can be deprived of your money,
your job and your home
by someone else,
but remember that
no one can ever take away your honor.

WILLIAM LYON PHELPS

Whatever you lend
let it be your money,
and not your name.
Money you may get again,
and, if not,
you may contrive to do without it;
name once lost you cannot get again,
and, if you cannot contrive
to do without it,
you had better never have been born.

EDWARD GEORGE BULWER-LYTTON

CONFIDENCE

A helping word
to one in trouble
is often like a switch
on a railroad track—
an inch between wreck
and smoothrolling prosperity.

HENRY WARD BEECHER

Don't let life discourage you;
everyone who got where he is
had to begin where he was.

RICHARD L. EVANS

Happy are those
who dream dreams
and are ready to pay the price
to make them come true.

LEON J. SUENENS

If one advances confidently
in the direction of his dreams,
and endeavors to live the life
which he has imagined,
he will meet with a success
unexpected in common hours.

HENRY DAVID THOREAU

———

Invest in yourself—
if you have confidence
in yourself.

WILLIAM FEATHER

———

Let no feeling of discouragement
prey upon you,
and in the end
you are sure to succeed.

ABRAHAM LINCOLN

Man must be arched
and buttressed from within,
else the temple will crumble to dust.

MARCUS AURELIUS

Mistakes occur
when a man is over-worked
or over-confident.

WILLIAM FEATHER

So long as a man
enjoys prosperity,
he cares not
whether he is beloved.

LUCAN

True prosperity
is the result of well placed confidence
in ourselves and our fellow man.

BENJAMIN BURT

We grow great by dreams.
All big men are dreamers.
They see things in the soft haze
of a spring day or in the red fire
of a long winter's evening.
Some of us let these great dreams die,
but others nourish and protect them,
nurse them through bad days
till they bring them
to the sunshine and light
which come always to those
who sincerely hope that their dreams
will come true.

WOODROW WILSON

When you affirm big,
believe big, and pray big,
big things happen.

NORMAN VINCENT PEALE

You all have powers
you never dreamed of.
You can do things
you never thought you could do.
There are no limitations
in what you can do
except the limitations
in your own mind
as to what you cannot do.
Don't think you *cannot*.
Think you *can*.

DAVID P. KINGSLEY

Blow your own horn loud.
If you succeed,
people will forgive your noise;
if you fail,
they'll forget it.

WILLIAM FEATHER

———

Every man
who believes in himself,
no matter who he be,
stands on a higher level
than the wobbler.

HERMANN KEYSERLING

———

To grow and to know
what one is growing towards—
that is the source of all strength
and confidence in life.

JAMES BAILLIE

If you think about disaster,
you will get it.
Brood about death
and you hasten your demise.
Think positively and masterfully,
with confidence and faith,
and life becomes more secure,
more fraught with action,
richer in achievement and experience.

EDWARD RICKENBACKER

ENDEAVOR

A job becomes work
only when you worry about it.

JOSEPHINE SCHAEFER

All growth depends upon activity.
There is no development
physically or intellectually
without effort,
and effort means work.
Work is not a curse;
it is the prerogative of intelligence,
the only means to manhood,
and the measure of civilization.

CALVIN COOLIDGE

Employment gives health,
sobriety, and morals.
Constant employment
and well-paid labor produce,
in a country like ours,
general prosperity,
content, and cheerfulness.

DANIEL WEBSTER

I have learned
that success is to be measured
not so much by the position
that one has reached in life
as by the obstacles
which he has overcome
while trying to succeed.

BOOKER T. WASHINGTON

If we would have anything of benefit,
we must earn it,
and earning it become shrewd,
inventive, ingenious, active, enterprising.

HENRY WARD BEECHER

If you have nothing else to do,
look about you and see
if there isn't something close at hand
that you can improve!
It may make you wealthy,
though it is more likely
that it will make you happy.

GEORGE MATTHEW ADAMS

Money never starts an idea;
it is the idea
that starts the money.

W. J. CAMERON

If your business keeps you so busy
that you have no time
for anything else,
there must be something wrong,
either with you
or with your business.

WILLIAM J. H. BOETCKER

In the democratic way of life
it is not
"the best things in life are free,"
but rather
"the best things in life
are worth working for!"

RUTH M. LEVERTON

Lampis the shipowner,
on being asked how he acquired
his great wealth, replied,
"My great wealth was acquired
with no difficulty,
but my small wealth,
my first gains,
with much labor."

EPICTETUS

———

Occupation is the necessary basis
of all enjoyment.

LEIGH HUNT

———

The busy man
has few idle visitors;
to the boiling pot
the flies come not.

BENJAMIN FRANKLIN

The conditions of conquest
are always easy.
We have but to toil awhile,
endure awhile,
believe always,
and never turn back.

SENECA

The reason American cities
are prosperous
is that there is no place
for people to sit down.

ALFRED J. TALLEY

The way to be nothing
is to do nothing.

EDGAR W. HOWE

The toughest thing about success
is that you've got to keep on being a success.
Talent is only a starting point in business.
You've got to keep working that talent.

IRVING BERLIN

—— ⋙⋘ ——

There are three things
which make a nation great and prosperous—
a fertile soil, busy workshops,
and easy conveyance
for men and commodities.

FRANCIS BACON

—— ⋙⋘ ——

To prosper soundly in business,
you must satisfy not only your customers,
but you must lay yourself out
to satisfy also the men who make
your product and the men who sell it.

HARRY BASSETT

FAME

Fame usually comes to those
who are thinking about
something else.

OLIVER WENDELL HOLMES

———⊰⊱———

Happy is the man
who hath never known
what it is to taste of fame—
to have it is a purgatory,
to want it is a hell.

EDWARD GEORGE BULWER-LYTTON

———⊰⊱———

He who would acquire fame
must not show himself
afraid of censure.
The dread of censure
is the death of genius.

WILLIAM SIMMS

How men long for celebrity!
Some would willingly
sacrifice their lives for fame,
and not a few
would rather be known
by their crimes
than not known at all.

JOHN SINCLAIR

If thou wilt receive profit,
read with humility,
simplicity and faith,
and seek not at any time
the fame of being learned.

THOMAS À KEMPIS

In fame's temple
there is always to be found
a niche for rich dunces,
importunate scoundrels,
or successful butchers
of the human race.

JOHANN ZIMMERMAN

Popularity disarms envy
in well-disposed minds.
Those are ever the most ready
to do justice to others,
who feel that the world
has done them justice.

WILLIAM HAZLITT

The delicate balance
between modesty and conceit
is popularity.

ROBERT HALF

———◦∘◦———

The fame of men
ought always to be estimated
by the means used
to acquire it.

FRANÇOIS LA ROCHEFOUCAULD

———◦∘◦———

The wise man
thinks of fame just enough
to avoid being despised.

EPICURUS

Wood burns
because it has the proper stuff in it;
and a man becomes famous
because he has the proper stuff
in him.

JOHANN WOLFGANG VON GOETHE

FAMILY

A child is a person
who is going to carry on
what you have started . . .
the fate of humanity
is in his hands.

ABRAHAM LINCOLN

A father is a banker
provided by nature.

FRENCH PROVERB

A man cannot leave
a better legacy to the world
than a well-educated family.

THOMAS SCOTT

As are families,
so is society.
If well ordered, well instructed,
and well governed,
they are the springs
from which go forth
the streams of national greatness
and prosperity—
of civil order and public happiness.

FRANK THAYER

Family life is the source
of the greatest human happiness.
This happiness is the simplest
and least costly kind,
and it cannot be purchased
with money.

ROBERT J. HAVIGHURST

Few fathers care much
for their sons,
or at least,
most of them care more
for their money.
Of those who really love their sons,
few know how to do it.

LORD CHESTERFIELD

(PHILIP DORMER STANHOPE)

I regard no man as poor
who has a godly mother.

ABRAHAM LINCOLN

How pleasant it is
for a father to sit
at his child's board.
It is like an aged man
reclining under the shadow
of an oak which he has planted.

SIR WALTER SCOTT

I believe the recipe for happiness
to be just enough money
to pay the monthly bills you acquire,
a little surplus
to give you confidence,
a little too much work each day,
enthusiasm for your work,
a substantial share of good health,
a couple of real friends,
and a wife and children
to share life's beauty with you.

J. KENFIELD MORLEY

No worldly success
can compensate
for failure in the home.

DAVID O. McKAY

Take the word "family."
Strike out the "m"
for mother and the "y" for youth—
and all you have left is "fail."

OMAR BURLESON

Woman knows
what Man has too long forgotten,
that the ultimate economic
and spiritual unit
of any civilization
is still the family.

CLARE BOOTH LUCE

In a family argument,
if it turns out you are right,
apologize at once!

ROBERT A. HEINLEIN

───≫●≪───

Let us be brothers—
or I'll cut your throat.

ECOUCHARD LEBRUN-PINDARE

───≫●≪───

Most men live
beyond women,
but often clinging to them
the while;
most women live
through men,
but not necessarily
in their behalf.

LOUIS KRONENBERGER

We inherit our relatives
and our features
and may not escape them;
but we can select our clothing
and our friends,
and let us be careful
that both fit us.

VOLNEY STREAMER

FORTUNE

A man who gives his children
habits of industry
provides for them
better than by giving them
a fortune.

RICHARD WHATELY

A man's felicity
consists not in the outward
and visible blessing
of fortune,
but in the inward
and unseen perfections
and riches of the mind.

ANARCHARSIS

I've been more bossed
by my fortune
than it has been
bossed by me.

JOHN P. LIPPETT

It is no good
making a fortune
if you do not know
how to enjoy it.
Higher material standards
are no good
if you do not know
how to use them for a better life.
Economic ideals
must include the
ideal of beauty
as well as the ideal of plenty.

SIR BASIL BLACKETT

If a man look sharply
and attentively,
he shall see Fortune;
for though she is blind,
she is not invisible.

FRANCIS BACON

It requires a great deal of boldness
and a great deal of caution
to make a great fortune;
and when you have got it,
it requires ten times as much wit
to keep it.

MEYER ROTHSCHILD

Never complain about your troubles;
they are responsible
for more than half of your income.

ROBERT UPDEGRAFF

Many have been ruined by their fortune,
and many have escaped ruin
by the want of fortune.
To obtain it
the great have become little,
and the little great.

JOHANN ZIMMERMAN

———

The brave man carves out his fortune,
and every man is the son of his own works.

MIGUEL DE CERVANTES

———

The use we make of our fortune
determines as to its sufficiency.
A little is enough if used wisely,
and too much
if expended foolishly.

CHRISTIAN BOVEE

The difficulties, hardships, and trials of life,
the obstacles one encounters
on the road to fortune,
are positive blessings.
They knit the muscles more firmly,
and teach self-reliance.
Peril is the element
in which power is developed.

WILLIAM MATTHEWS

The surplus wealth we have gained
to some extent at least
belongs to our fellow beings;
we are only the temporary custodians
of our fortunes,
and let us be careful
that no just complaint can be made
against our stewardship.

JACOB H. SCHIFF

FRIENDSHIP

But for money and the need of it,
there would not be half the friendship
in the world.
It is powerful for good
if divinely used.
Give it plenty of air
and it is sweet as the hawthorn;
shut it up and it cankers
and breeds worms.

GEORGE MACDONALD

Every organism
requires an environment of friends,
partly to shield it from violent changes,
and partly to supply it
with its wants.

ALFRED NORTH WHITEHEAD

Friends are an aid to the young,
to guard them from error;
to the elderly, to attend to their wants
and to supplement their failing power of action;
to those in the prime of life,
to assist them to noble deeds.

ARISTOTLE

Friendship is the only cement
that will ever hold
the world together.

WOODROW WILSON

In prosperity it is very easy
to find a friend;
in adversity,
nothing is so difficult.

EPICTETUS

It is a good thing
to be rich,
it is a good thing
to be strong,
but it is a better thing
to be beloved
of many friends.

EURIPIDES

It is great to have friends
when one is young,
but indeed it is still more so
when you are getting old.
When we are young,
friends are, like everything else,
a matter of course.
In the old days we know
what it means to have them.

EDVARD GRIEG

No one is rich enough
to do without a neighbor.

DANISH PROVERB

The holy passion of Friendship
is of so sweet and steady
and loyal and enduring a nature
that it will last
through a whole lifetime,
if not asked to lend money.

MARK TWAIN

The making of friends
who are real friends,
is the best token we have
of a man's success in life.

EDWARD B. HALE

Years and years of happiness
only make us realize
how lucky we are
to have friends that have shared
and made that happiness a reality.

ROBERT E. FREDERICK

The friend of my adversity
I shall always cherish most.
I can better trust those
who helped to relieve the gloom
of my dark hours
than those who are so ready
to enjoy with me the sunshine
of my prosperity.

ULYSSES S. GRANT

GENEROSITY

A man there was,
and they called him mad;
the more he gave,
the more he had.

JOHN BUNYAN

A man's true wealth
is the good he does
in this world.

MOHAMMED

A really great man
is known by three signs—
generosity in the design,
humanity in the execution,
moderation in success.

OTTO EDWARD BISMARK

A rich man
who consecrates his wealth
and his position
to the good of humanity
is a success.
A poor man
who gives of his service
and his sympathy to others
has achieved true success
even though material prosperity
or outward honors
never come to him.

NORMAN VINCENT PEALE

Almost always
the most indigent
are the most generous.

KING STANISLAUS OF POLAND

Avarice, in old age, is foolish;
for what can be more absurd
than to increase our provisions
for the road the nearer we approach
to our journey's end?

CICERO

It is better to give
than to lend,
and it costs about the same.

SIR PHILLIP GIBBS

Generosity during life
is a very different thing
from generosity in the hour of death;
one proceeds from genuine liberality
and benevolence,
the other from pride or fear.

HORACE MANN

Be busy in trading,
receiving, and giving,
for life is too good
to be wasted in living.

JOHN STERLING

Happiness is not so much
in having or sharing.
We make a living
by what we get,
but we make a life
by what we give.

NORMAN MACEWAN

Money is like muck,
not good unless spread.

FRANCIS BACON

I would have a man
generous to his country,
his neighbors, his kindred,
his friends, and most of all
his poor friends.
Not like some
who are most lavish
with those who are able
to give most to them.

PLINY

Money spent on ourselves
may be a millstone
about the neck;
spent on others it may
give us wings like eagles.

RAYMOND HITCHCOCK

Money was made
for the free-hearted and generous.

JOHN RAY

No person was ever honored
for what he received.
Honor has been the reward
for what he gave.

CALVIN COOLIDGE

The life of a man consists
not in seeing visions
and in dreaming dreams,
but in active charity
and in willing service.

HENRY WADSWORTH LONGFELLOW

The old thought
that one cannot be rich
except at the expense
of his neighbor,
must pass away.
True prosperity
adds to the richness
of the whole world,
such as that of the man
who makes two trees grow
where only one grew before.

ANNE RIX MILTZ

⎯⎯⎯⎯

They who give
have all things;
they who withhold
have nothing.

HINDU PROVERB

To rejoice in the prosperity
of another
is to partake of it.

WILLIAM AUSTIN

⟶✦⟵

Watch lest prosperity
destroy generosity.

HENRY WARD BEECHER

⟶✦⟵

We enjoy thoroughly
only the pleasure that we give.

ALEXANDRE DUMAS

We need to be just
before we are generous,
as we need shirts
before ruffles.

SÉBASTIEN CHAMFORT

GREATNESS

Adversity
has made many a man great
who, had he remained prosperous,
would only have been rich.

MAURICE SWITZER

All greatness is unconscious,
or it is little and naught.

THOMAS CARLYLE

Every one has a fair turn
to be as great as he pleases.

JEREMY COLLIER

Greatness lies not in being strong,
but in the right using of strength.

HENRY WARD BEECHER

If thou art rich,
then show the greatness
of thy fortune;
or what is better,
the greatness of thy soul,
in the meekness
of thy conversation;
condescend to men of low estate,
support the distressed,
and patronize the neglected.
Be great.

LAURENCE STERNE

In prosperity
let us particularly avoid pride,
disdain and arrogance.

CICERO

It has always been a crime
to be above the crowd.
That's the real reason
why some men in public life
are maligned, attacked
and slandered,
for they are beyond the reach
of those who realize
in their own heart
that the greatness of others
shows their own smallness,
their own inferiority.

WILLIAM J. H. BOETCKER

Prosperity
is the surest breeder
of insolence I know.

MARK TWAIN

Putting oneself in the limelight
at the expense of others
is a wrong idea
of greatness.
The secret of greatness
rather than bigness
is to acclimate oneself
to one's place of service
and be true to one's own convictions.
A life of this kind of service
will forever remain
the measure of one's true greatness.

RICHARD W. SHELLY JR.

The most substantial glory of a country
is in its virtuous great men.
Its prosperity will depend
on its docility
to learn from their example.

FISHER AMES

True greatness,
first of all,
is a thing of the heart.
It is alive with robust
and generous sympathies.
It is neither behind its age
nor too far before it.
It is up with its age,
and ahead of it only just so far
as to be able to lead its march.
It cannot slumber,
for activity is a necessity
of its existence.
It is no reservoir, but a fountain.

ROSWELL D. HITCHCOCK

He that can heroically endure adversity
will bear prosperity
with equal greatness of soul;
for the mind that cannot be dejected
by the former
is not likely to be transported
with the latter.

HENRY FIELDING

It isn't
what you make . . .
it's what you do
with what you make.

RALPH A. HAYWARD

The riches we impart
are the only wealth
we shall always retain

MATTHEW HENRY

To be great
is to be
misunderstood.

RALPH WALDO EMERSON

HAPPINESS

Fate often puts all the material
for happiness and prosperity
into a man's hands
just to see how miserable
he can make himself with them.

DON MARQUIS

Happiness is a hard thing
because it is achieved
only by making others happy.

STUART CLOETE

Happiness is not perfected
until it is shared.

JANE PORTER

Happiness?
That's nothing more
than good health
and a poor memory.

ALBERT SCHWEITZER

Happy is he
who has laid up in his youth,
and held fast in all fortune,
a genuine and passionate
love for reading.

RUFUS CHOATE

He is a man of sense
who does not grieve
for what he has not,
but rejoices in what he has.

EPICTETUS

If this world afford true happiness,
it is to be found in a home
where love and confidence
increase with the years,
where the necessities of life
come without severe strain,
where luxuries enter
only after their cost
has been carefully considered.

A. EDWARD NEWTON

It's good to have money
and the things that money can buy,
but it's good, too,
to check up once in a while
and make sure that you haven't lost
the things that money can't buy.

GEORGE HORACE LORIMER

Joy is spiritual prosperity.
That motto above your desk—
"Smile!"
How did that ever get into
so many business offices?
Does a smile help business?
Try it. Joy makes the face shine,
and he that hath a merry heart
hath a continual feast.

W. C. ISETT

Money never made a man happy yet,
nor will it.
There is nothing in its nature
to produce happiness.

BENJAMIN FRANKLIN

No social system
will bring us happiness,
health and prosperity
unless it is inspired
by something greater
than materialism.

CLEMENT R. ATTLEE

⎯•=•⎯

The happiest people
are those who are too busy
to notice whether they are or not.

WILLIAM FEATHER

⎯•=•⎯

The happy people
are those who are producing something;
the bored people are those
who are consuming much
and producing nothing.

WILLIAM RALPH INGE

True life is possible
in social conditions the most diverse,
and with natural gifts the most unequal.
It is not fortune
or personal advantage,
but our turning them to account,
that constitutes the value of life.
Fame adds no more
than does length of days;
quality is the thing.

CHARLES WAGNER

You never see
the stock called Happiness
quoted on the exchange.

HENRY VAN DYKE

Moderate desires
constitute a character
fitted to acquire all the good
which the world can yield.
He who has this character
is prepared,
in whatever situation he is,
therewith to be content;
has learned the science
of being happy;
and possesses the alchemic stone
which changes every metal
into gold.

TIMOTHY DWIGHT

Happiness is a dividend
on a well-invested life.

DUNCAN STUART

HEALTH

For health
and the constant enjoyment of life,
give me a keen and ever present sense of humor;
it is the next best thing
to an abiding faith in providence.

GEORGE B. CHEEVER

He who has health,
has hope;
and he who has hope,
has everything.

ARABIAN PROVERB

Health is so necessary
to all the duties,
as well as pleasures of life,
that the crime of squandering it
is equal to the folly.

SAMUEL JOHNSON

Life is growth—
a challenge of environment.
If we cannot meet
our everyday surroundings
with equanimity and pleasure
and grow each day
in some useful direction,
then this splendid balance
of cosmic forces
which we call life
is on the road toward misfortune,
misery and destruction.
Therefore, health is the most precious
of all things.

LUTHER BURBANK

Look to your health;
and if you have it . . .
value it next to a good conscience,
for health is the second blessing
that we mortals are capable of—
a blessing that money cannot buy.

IZAAK WALTON

People who are always taking care
of their health are like misers,
who are hoarding up a treasure
which they have never spirit enough
to enjoy.

LAURENCE STERNE

Protect your health.
Without it you face a serious handicap
for success and happiness.

HARRY F. BANKS

The health of nations
is more important
than the wealth of nations.

WILL DURANT

The only way
for a rich man to be healthy
is by exercise and abstinence,
to live as if he were poor.

SIR WILLIAM TEMPLE

What have I gained
by health?
Intolerable dullness.
What by moderate meals?
A total blank.

CHARLES LAMB

Without health,
life is not life;
it is only a state
of languor and suffering—
an image of death.

FRANÇOIS RABELAIS

Worry affects the circulation,
the heart, the glands,
the whole nervous system,
and profoundly affects
the health.
I have never known a man
who died from overwork,
but many who died from doubt.

CHARLES W. MAYO

Liberty is to the collective body,
what health is
to every individual body.
Without health
no pleasure can be tasted
by man;
without liberty,
no happiness can be enjoyed
by society.

LORD BOLINGBROKE

(HENRY ST. JOHN)

Not the state of the body
but the state of the mind and soul
is the measure of the wellbeing
of each of us.

WINFRED RHOADES

There is no exercise
better for the heart
than reaching down
and lifting people up.

JOHN ANDREW HOLMES

Wealth is a means to an end,
not an end itself.
As a synonym for health and happiness,
it has had a fair trial
and failed dismally.

JOHN GALSWORTHY

$\mathcal{K}$NOWLEDGE

If a man empties his purse
into his head,
no one can take it away from him.
An investment in knowledge
always pays the best interest.

BENJAMIN FRANKLIN

It is the glorious prerogative
of the empire of knowledge
that what it gains it never loses.
On the contrary,
it increases by the multiple
of its own power:
all its ends become means;
all its attainments
help to new conquests.

DANIEL WEBSTER

Knowledge cannot be stolen from us.
It cannot be bought or sold.
We may be poor,
and the sheriff may come
and sell our furniture,
or drive away our cow,
or take our pet lamb,
and leave us homeless and penniless;
but he cannot lay the law's hand
upon the jewelry of our minds.

ELIHU BURRITT

Knowledge comes by eyes
always open and working hand,
and there is no knowledge that is not power.

JEREMY TAYLOR

Knowledge is a treasure
but practice is the key to it.

THOMAS FULLER

Knowledge is the treasure,
but judgment is the treasurer
of a wise man.

WILLIAM PENN

Learning, like money,
may be of so base a coin
as to be utterly void of use;
or, if sterling,
may require good management
to make it serve
the purposes of sense
or happiness.

WILLIAM SHENSTONE

They say that knowledge
is power.
I used to think so,
but I now know
that they meant money.
Every guinea
is a philosopher's stone.

LORD BYRON

(GEORGE GORDON)

———

Thinking leads a man
to knowledge.
He may see and hear, and read and learn
whatever he pleases,
and as much as he pleases;
he will never know anything of it,
except as he has thought it over . . .
By thinking he has made it the property
of his own mind.

JOHANN PESTALOZZI

What a different world this would be
if people would listen
to those who know more
and not merely try to get something
from those who have more.

WILLIAM J. H. BOETCKER

What you have come to know,
pursue by exercise;
what you have not learned,
seek to add to your knowledge,
for it is as reprehensible
to hear a profitable saying and not grasp it
as to be offered a good gift by one's friends
and not accept it.
Believe that many precepts
are better than much wealth,
for wealth quickly fails us,
but precepts abide through all time.

ISOCRATES

LEISURE

He that will make good use
of any part of his life
must allow a large part of it
to recreation.

JOHN LOCKE

If ever this free people,
if this government itself
is ever utterly demoralized,
it will come from this human wiggle
and struggle for office—
that is, a way to live without work.

ABRAHAM LINCOLN

Increased means
and increased leisure
arethe two civilizers of man.

BENJAMIN DISRAELI

It is impossible to enjoy
idling thoroughly
unless one has plenty of work to do.

JEROME K. JEROME

———

It is the genius of the summer
to restore to us the Golden Age
when men lay lazily
under the trees,
and crimson-cheeked fruits
fell all around them
with a plump,
so that they had not even
to take the trouble
to rise out of their lethargy
in order to pick them.

ROBERT LYND

Leisure and solitude
are the best effect of riches,
because they are the mother of thought.
Both are avoided
by most rich men
who seek company and business,
which are signs of being weary
of themselves.

SIR WILLIAM TEMPLE

Leisure for men of business,
and business for men of leisure,
would cure many complaints.

HESTER THRALE

Rest has cured more people
than all the medicine
in the world.

HAROLD J. REILLY

Rest is a fine medicine.
Let your stomachs rest,
ye dyspeptics;
let your brain rest,
you wearied and worried
men of business;
let your limbs rest,
ye children of toil!

THOMAS CARLYLE

Some relaxation is necessary
to people of every degree;
the head that thinks
and the hand that labors
must have some little time
to recruit their diminished powers.

BERNARD GILPIN

Temptation rarely comes
in working hours.
It is in their leisure time
that men are made or marred.

WILLIAM M. TAYLOR

The more we do,
the more we can do;
the more busy we are,
the more leisure we have.

WILLIAM HAZLITT

Wealth may be
an excellent thing,
for it means power,
leisure and liberty.

JAMES RUSSELL LOWELL

The walking-stick
serves the purpose of an advertisement
that the bearer's hands
are employed otherwise
than in useful effort,
and it therefore has utility
as an evidence of leisure.

THORSTEIN VEBLEN

To be able to fill leisure intelligently
is the last product of civilization.

BERTRAND RUSSELL

Waste of time
is the most extravagant
of all expense.

THEOPHRASTUS

It is curious how tyrannical
the habit of reading is,
and what shifts we make
to escape thinking.
There is no bore
we dread being left alone with
so much as our own minds.

JAMES RUSSELL LOWELL

———

There's no music in "rest,"
but there's the making of music in it.
And people are always missing
that part of the life melody,
always talking of perseverance
and courage and fortitude,
but patience is the finest
and worthiest part of fortitude,
and the rarest, too.

JOHN RUSKIN

LUXURY

A man should inure himself
to voluntary labor,
and not give up
to indulgence and pleasure,
as they beget no good constitution
of body nor knowledge
of mind.

SOCRATES

———

Every luxury must be paid for,
and everything is a luxury,
starting with being in the world.

CESARE PAVESE

———

Indulge yourself in pleasures
only in so far as they are necessary
for the preservation of health.

SPINOZA

It happens a little unluckily
that the persons
who have the most infinite contempt
of money are the same
that have the strongest appetite
for the pleasures it procures.

WILLIAM SHENSTONE

Luxury is the first,
second and third cause
of the ruin of republics.
It is the vampire
which soothes us
into a fatal slumber
while it sucks the life-blood
of our veins.

PAYSON

Luxury makes a man so soft
that it is hard to please him,
and easy to trouble him;
so that his pleasures at last
become his burden.
Luxury is a nice master,
hard to be pleased.

MACKENZIE

Most of the luxuries,
and many of the so-called
comforts of life
are not only indispensible,
but positive hindrances
to the elevation of mankind.

HENRY DAVID THOREAU

One of the greatest pleasures
to be derived from wealth
in any form
is the delight inherent
in choosing the proper vocational program
for one's life . . .
The man who selects
the proper vocation in life
has all the luxuries
that life can provide.

LLOYD E. BOUGHAM

The use of money
is all the advantage
there is in having money.

BENJAMIN FRANKLIN

Though a taste of pleasure
may quicken the relish of life,
an unrestrained indulgence
leads to inevitable destruction.

DODSLEY

———◦◦◦———

For me,
hard work represents
the supreme luxury of life.

ALBERT M. GREENFIELD

———◦◦◦———

Possessions, outward success,
publicity, luxury—
to me these have always been contemptible.
I believe that a simple and unassuming
manner of life
is best for everyone,
best both for the body and the mind.

ALBERT EINSTEIN

If this world
affords true happiness,
it is to be found in a home
where love and confidence
increase with the years,
where the necessities of life
come without severe strain,
where luxuries enter
only after their cost
has been carefully considered.

A. EDWARD NEWTON

Surplus wealth
is a sacred trust
which its possessor
is bound to administer
in his lifetime
for the good of the community.

ANDREW CARNEGIE

To have read the greatest works
of any great poet,
to have beheld or heard
the greatest works
of any great painter or musician,
is a possession added
to the best things of life.

ALGERNON SWINBURNE

We rich men
count our happiness
to lie in the little superfluities,
not in necessities.

PLUTARCH

OPPORTUNITY

I make the most
of all that comes,
and the least
of all that goes.

SARA TEASDALE

⁓✦⁓

If we are to achieve
a victorious standard of living today
we must look for the opportunity
in every difficulty
instead of being paralyzed
at the thought of the difficulty
in every opportunity.

WALTER E. COLE

⁓✦⁓

Opportunity has power
over all things.

SOPHOCLES

It is less important
to redistribute wealth
than it is
to redistribute opportunity.

ARTHUR H. VANDENBURG

Life is a long line
of opportunities.
Wealth is not in making money,
but in making the man
while he is making money.
Production, not destruction,
leads to success.

JOHN WICKER

The first man
gets the oyster,
the second man
gets the shell.

ANDREW CARNEGIE

The sure way
to miss success
is to miss
the opportunity.

VICTOR CHASLES

What is opportunity
to the man who can't use it?
An unfecunded egg,
which the waves of time
wash away into nonentity.

GEORGE ELIOT

The true way to gain much,
is never to desire
to gain too much.
He is not rich
that possesses much,
but he that covets no more;
and he is not poor
that enjoys little,
but he that wants too much.

FRANCIS BEAUMONT

To be a great man
it is necessary
to turn to account
all opportunities.

FRANÇOIS LA ROCHEFOUCAULD

To every man his chance,
to every man,
regardless of his birth,
his shining golden opportunity.
To every man the right to live,
to work, to be himself,
and to become whatever thing
his manhood and his vision
can contribute to make him.

THOMAS WOLFE

SECURITY

Big business can't prosper
without small business
to supply its needs
and buy its products.
Labor can't prosper
so long as capital lies idle.
Capital can't prosper
while labor is unemployed.

DEWITT EMERY

In prosperity, caution;
in adversity, patience.

DUTCH PROVERB

Prosperity is only
an instrument to be used,
not a deity
to be worshipped.

CALVIN COOLIDGE

Let us keep a firm grip
upon our money,
for without it
the whole assembly of virtues
are but as blades of grass.

BHATRIHARI

Many persons think
that by hoarding money
they are gaining safety
for themselves.
If money is your only hope
for independence,
you will never have it.
The only real security
that a man can have in this world
is a reserve of knowledge,
experience and ability.

HENRY FORD

Money is a guarantee
that we may have what we want
in the future.
Though we need nothing
at the moment
it insures the possibility
of satisfying a new desire
when it arises.

ARISTOTLE

The lesson which wars
and depressions have taught
is that if we want peace,
prosperity and happiness at home
we must help to establish them abroad.

HUGO L. BLACK

The trouble with worrying so much
about your "security" in the future
is that you feel so insecure
in the present.

HARLAN MILLER

To acquire wealth
is not easy,
yet to keep it
is even more difficult . . .
It is said
that wealth is like a viper
which is harmless
if a man know
how to take hold of it;
but, if he does not,
it will twine around his hand
and bite him.

FRANK K. HOUSTON

Too many people
are thinking of security
instead of opportunity.
They seem more afraid
of life than of death.

JAMES F. BYRNES

With labor and management
working together in common cause—
and not against each other—
we can build and produce and prosper,
and defeat any threat,
from whatever source,
against our own security
and the peace of the world.

WILLIAM GREEN

THRIFT

A man who both spends
and saves money
is the happiest man,
because he has both enjoyments.

SAMUEL JOHNSON

⟶⟶⟶

All the money in the world
is no use to a man
or his country
if he spends it
as fast as he makes it.
All he has left is his bills
and the reputation
for being a fool.

RUDYARD KIPLING

⟶⟶⟶

Ask thy purse
what thou should spend.

SCOTTISH PROVERB

Economy is half the battle of life;
it is not so hard to earn money
as to spend it well.

CHARLES SPURGEON

I would rather be a beggar
and spend my money like a king,
than be a king
and spend money like a beggar.

ROBERT G. INGERSOLL

I would rather have people laugh
at my economies
than weep for my extravagance.

KING OSCAR II OF SWEDEN

In moderating,
not in satisfying desires,
lies peace.

REGINALD HEBER

More people
should learn to tell their dollars
where to go
instead of asking them
where they went.

ROGER BABSON

Open your mouth
and purse cautiously,
and your stock of wealth and reputation
shall, at least in repute, be great.

ZIMMERMANN

People who never had
enough thrift and forethought
to buy and pay for property
in the first place
seldom have enough
to keep the property up
after they have gained it
in some other way.

THOMAS NIXON CARVER

To acquire wealth is difficult,
to preserve it more difficult,
but to spend it wisely
most difficult of all.

EDWARD DAY

Savings represent
much more than mere money value.
They are the proof
that the saver is worth something
in himself.
Any fool can waste;
any fool can muddle;
but it takes something
more of a man to save
and the more he saves
the more of a man he makes
of himself.

RUDYARD KIPLING

When prosperity comes,
do not use all of it.

CONFUCIUS

In short, the way to wealth,
if you desire it,
is as plain as the way to market.
It depends chiefly on two words,
industry and *frugality*;
that is, waste neither *time* nor *money*,
but make the best use of both.

BENJAMIN FRANKLIN

You cannot bring about prosperity
by discouraging thrift . . .
You cannot lift the wage-earner
by pulling down the wage-payer . . .
You cannot keep out of trouble
by spending more than your income.

WILLIAM J. H. BOETCKER

In adversity
assume the countenance
of prosperity,
and in prosperity
moderate the temper
and desires.

LIVY

———

What a man does with his wealth
depends upon his idea of happiness.
Those who draw prizes in life
are apt to spend tastelessly,
if not viciously,
not knowing that it requires
as much talent to spend
as to make.

EDWIN P. WHIPPLE

WEALTH

Budgets are not merely
affairs of arithmetic,
but in a thousand ways
go to the root of prosperity
of individuals,
the relation of classes
and the strength of kingdoms.

WILLIAM E. GLADSTONE

Genuine morality is preserved
only in the school of adversity;
a state of continuous prosperity
may easily prove
a quicksand to virtue.

JOHANN SCHILLER

Gold is the most useless thing
in the world.
I am not interested in money
but in the things of
which money is merely a symbol.

HENRY FORD

Great spenders
are bad lenders.

BENJAMIN FRANKLIN

He that is proud of riches
is a fool.
For if he be exalted
above his neighbors
because he hath more gold,
how much inferior is he
to a gold mine.

JEREMY TAYLOR

If we command our wealth,
we shall be rich and free;
if our wealth commands us,
we are poor indeed.

EDMUND BURKE

If you want to know
how rich you really are,
find out what would be
left of you tomorrow
if you should lose every dollar
you own tonight?

WILLIAM J. H. BOETCKER

It is much better
to have your gold in the hand
than in the heart.

CHARLES CALEB COLTON

It is where a man
spends his money
that shows where his heart lies.

A. EDWIN KEIGWIN

———

Many people
take no care of their money
till they come nearly to the end of it,
and others do just the same
with their time.

JOHANN WOLFGANG VON GOETHE

———

Money is a stupid measure
of achievement
but unfortunately
it is the only universal measure
we have.

CHARLES P. STEINMETZ

Money may be
the husk of many things,
but not the kernel.
It brings you food,
but not appetite;
medicine,
but not health;
acquaintance,
but not friends;
servants,
but not loyalty;
days of joy,
but not peace or happiness.

HENRIK IBSEN

Of all the advantages
which come to any young man,
I believe it to be demonstrably true
that poverty is the greatest.

JOSEPH G. HOLLAND

Property may be destroyed
and money may lose
its purchasing power, but,
character, health, knowledge
and good judgment
will always be in demand
under all conditions.

ROGER BABSON

When a man says
money can do anything,
that settles it: he hasn't any.

EDGAR W. HOWE

Prosperity is too apt
to prevent us from examining
our conduct;
but adversity leads us to think
properly of our state,
and so is most beneficial to us.

SAMUEL JOHNSON

Some of the proudest
and most arrogant people
I have known
were morons and paupers,
while some of the most wonderful and humble
were wealthy.

F. HOWARD CALLAHAN

The darkest hour
in the history of any young man
is when he sits down
to study how to get money
without honestly earning it.

HORACE GREELEY

Wealth is a dangerous inheritance,
unless the inheritor is trained
to active benevolence.

CHARLES SIMMONS

Wealth is not only
what you have
but it is also
what you are.

STERLING W. SILL

When men are so busy
making money
that they have no time
for anything else,
then the day is not far off
when they will have no money
for anything else.

WILLIAM J. H. BOETCKER

INDEX